# About
# Skill Builders
# Word Problems

## by Carolyn Chapman

**W**elcome to Rainbow Bridge Publishing's Skill Builders series. Like our Summer Bridge Activities collection, the Skill Builders series is designed to make learning fun and rewarding.

Students often ask parents and teachers, "When am I ever going to use this?" Skill Builders *Word Problems* was developed to help students see the uses of math in the world around them. Exercises help students develop problem-solving skills in real-world situations while increasing confidence in their math skills.

Content is based on NCTM (National Council of Teachers of Mathematics) standards and supports what teachers are currently using in their classrooms. Word Problems can be used both at school and at home to engage students in problem solving.

The fourth-grade math skills used in this book include addition, subtraction, multiplication, division, reading graphs, fractions, measurement, area and perimeter, money values, and decimals. Special emphasis is given to multistep problems.

A critical thinking section includes exercises to help develop higher-order thinking skills.

Learning is more effective when approached with an element of fun and enthusiasm. That's why the Skill Builders combine academically-sound exercises with engaging graphics and themes—to make reviewing basic skills fun and effective.

# Table of Contents

Solve each problem.

---

Anita saw 25 grasshoppers and 16 beetles in the field. How many grasshoppers and beetles did Anita see altogether?

$$\begin{array}{r} \overset{1}{\mathbf{25}} \\ + \ \mathbf{16} \\ \hline \mathbf{41} \ \textbf{bugs} \end{array}$$

---

**1.** Charley counted 19 more black ants than red ants. Charley counted 34 red ants. How many black ants did Charley count?

**2.** There were 28 more caterpillars in the flower garden than in the vegetable garden. If there were 31 caterpillars in the vegetable garden, how many caterpillars were there in the flower garden?

---

**3.** Eric counted 13 black spiders and 48 brown spiders. How many spiders did Eric count altogether?

Bugs are so cool!

**4.** Jill saw 29 ladybugs in the orchard and 14 ladybugs near the patio. How many ladybugs did Jill see in all?

---

Word Problems Grade 4—RBP0717

# At the Zoo

Solve each problem.

Jackson fed the penguins 342 pounds of food in March. In May, Jackson fed the penguins 489 pounds of food. How many pounds of food did Jackson feed the penguins total?

1 1
**342**
**+ 489**
**831 pounds of food**

---

**1.** Laura counted 14 green lizards, 35 snakes, and 48 chameleons. How many reptiles did she see in all?

**2.** On Monday, 2,492 people visited the zoo. On Saturday, 4,399 people visited the zoo. How many people visited the zoo on Monday and Saturday altogether?

**3.** Alex took 34 pictures of bears, 29 pictures of cats, and 48 pictures of reptiles. How many pictures did Alex take altogether?

**4.** Kesha spoke to the zookeeper about what the birds are fed. The birds ate 3,295 ounces of birdseed in the spring and 2,945 ounces in the summer. How many ounces of birdseed did the birds eat in the spring and summer combined?

Solve each problem.

1. Adam saw 15 bees in the flowers. Later, Adam saw 22 bees in the flowers. How many bees did Adam see altogether?

2. Andy cleaned 45 cages on Monday, 36 cages on Tuesday, and 69 cages on Wednesday. How many cages did Andy clean altogether?

3. Marcy saw 21 more butterflies than Jim. Jim saw 19 butterflies. How many butterflies did Marcy see?

4. Lisa walked 72 feet to see the leopards, 129 feet to see the alligators, and 218 feet to see the monkeys. How many feet did Lisa walk in all?

**Did you know?**

In the U.S., 13 species of reptiles are on the endangered species list. Four of the 13 endangered species are sea turtles.

# How Tall?

Solve each problem.

The tallest giant sequoia tree is 275 feet.
The tallest coastal redwood tree is 321 feet.
How much taller is the coastal redwood
tree than the giant sequoia tree?

$$\begin{array}{r} 2^{1}11 \\ \cancel{321} \\ -\ 275 \\ \hline 46 \end{array}$$ **feet taller**

**1.** The Sears Tower in Chicago is 1,450 feet tall. The John Hancock Center in Chicago is 1,127 feet tall. How much taller is the Sears Tower than the John Hancock Center?

**2.** The tallest sugar pine tree is 232 feet. The tallest western red cedar tree is 159 feet. How much taller is the sugar pine than the western red cedar?

**3.** The Empire State Building is 1,250 feet tall. The Chrysler Building is 1,046 feet tall. How much taller is the Empire State Building than the Chrysler Building?

**4.** Both the Mauna Loa and Kilauea volcanoes are in Hawaii. The Mauna Loa volcano is 13,680 feet tall. The Kilauea volcano is 4,190 feet tall. How much taller is the Mauna Loa volcano than the Kilauea volcano?

# Under the Sea

Solve each problem.

Divers saw 432 tropical fish on their first dive, 289 tropical fish on their second dive, and 637 tropical fish on their third dive. How many tropical fish did they see altogether?

```
  1 1
  432
  289
+ 637
```
**1,358 tropical fish**

1. The Pacific Ocean has an average depth of 12,925 feet. The Gulf of Mexico has an average depth of 5,297 feet. What is the difference in average depth between the Gulf of Mexico and the Pacific Ocean?

2. Misha collected 1,946 seashells. Abe collected 3,479 seashells. How many seashells did Misha and Abe collect in all?

*I see the fish under the sea!*

3. A blue whale traveled 1,349 feet the first time it was sighted. The second time it was sighted, the blue whale had traveled another 977 feet. How far did the blue whale travel altogether?

4. A scientist observed 423 sea urchins on his first trip. On his second trip, the scientist observed 296 sea urchins. How many more sea urchins did the scientist observe on his first trip than on his second trip?

Word Problems Grade 4—RBP0717

Solve each problem.

**1.** Mount Everest, the world's tallest mountain, is 29,035 feet tall. Mount McKinley is 20,320 feet tall. How much taller is Mount Everest than Mount McKinley?

**2.** The California laurel tree is 108 feet tall. The Sitka spruce tree is 191 feet tall. How much taller is the Sitka spruce than the California laurel?

Gee whiz, Mr. Fredrickson, you're really tall!

**3.** Jason saw 42 squid, 142 crabs, and 339 fish. How many sea creatures did he see altogether?

**4.** Leslie saw 1,228 fewer fish than Taylor. Taylor saw 3,212 fish. How many fish did Leslie see?

**Did you know?**

The oldest living tree is in California. It is a bristlecone pine tree named Methuselah, and it is estimated to be over 4,600 years old.

© Rainbow Bridge Publishing

Solve each problem.

---

Paige saw 142 tourists in July, August, and September. She saw 32 tourists in July and 89 tourists in August. How many tourists did Paige see in September?

$$\begin{array}{r} \overset{1}{3}2 \\ +\ 89 \\ \hline 121 \end{array} \qquad \begin{array}{r} 142 \\ -\ 121 \\ \hline 21 \text{ tourists} \end{array}$$

---

**1.** Mario took pictures of 57 landmarks in the city he visited. He took 12 pictures of buildings, 16 pictures of bridges, and 2 pictures of statues. The rest were pictures of parks. How many pictures of parks did Mario take?

**2.** Ron drove 83 tourists altogether. Fifteen tourists had cameras. Twenty-two tourists had binoculars. How many tourists didn't have binoculars or cameras?

**3.** Jamie mailed 432 postcards in a week. She mailed 139 postcards on Monday and 54 postcards on Tuesday. How many postcards did she mail the rest of the week?

**4.** Derek bought 29 souvenirs. He gave 13 to his sister. Then, he bought 42 more. How many souvenirs does Derek have now?

9

Solve each problem.

1. Amelia works in a hotel. She carried 34 pieces of luggage on Tuesday and 49 pieces on Wednesday. If she carried 569 pieces of luggage during the week, how many pieces did she carry on the rest of the days?

2. Eight hundred eighty-one people visited the museum last year. There were 211 visitors during the summer, 124 visitors during the winter, and 389 visitors during the fall season. How many visitors did the museum have during the spring season?

3. Becky bought a poster from every city she visited. On her first trip, she bought 64 posters. On her second trip, she bought 183 posters. She gave 31 posters to her friend. How many posters does Becky have now?

4. Antonio traveled 992 miles in a week. He traveled 329 miles on Wednesday. On Thursday he traveled 410 miles. How many miles did Antonio travel the rest of the week?

**Did you know?**

It took the *Mayflower* 66 days to sail across the Atlantic Ocean from Plymouth, England, to America.

# Soap Suds

Solve each problem.

**1.** Mason works at a laundry. He uses 214 pounds of soap in January, 471 pounds in February, and 447 pounds in March. If Mason has 1,500 pounds of soap to start with, how many pounds of soap does he have left?

**2.** Dennis washes 390 socks altogether. He washes 42 blue socks, 16 green socks, 130 white socks, and 52 black socks. If the rest are brown, how many brown socks does he wash?

**3.** Elizabeth washes 12 loads of laundry on Monday, 14 loads on Tuesday, and 29 loads on Wednesday. If she washes 85 loads of laundry for the entire week, how many loads does she wash the rest of the week?

**4.** Kayla has 46 socks. She washes them and discovers she now has 32. On her way home she loses another 12 socks. How many socks did Kayla lose altogether?

### Did you know?

The washing machine was invented in 1901 by Langmuir Fisher.

Word Problems Grade 4—RBP0717

# School Lunch

Solve each problem using the information in the table.

Matt eats an orange, a peanut butter sandwich, and a glass of milk for lunch. How many calories does Matt eat?

$$
\begin{array}{r}
1 \\
1\,65 \\
334 \\
+\ 95 \\
\hline
494\ \textbf{calories}
\end{array}
$$

1. How many more calories does one slice of pizza have than a peanut butter sandwich?

2. If Lori eats a hamburger and one serving of celery for lunch, how many calories does she eat?

Tuna on rye—my favorite!

3. After school, Allie has chocolate chip cookies and a glass of milk for a snack. How many calories does she eat?

4. For lunch, Tanner orders a bowl of chicken noodle soup, applesauce, and chocolate chip cookies. How many calories are in his lunch?

| FOOD ITEMS | CALORIES | |
|---|---|---|
| applesauce | | 194 |
| celery | | 9 |
| chicken noodle soup | | 75 |
| chocolate chip cookies | | 226 |
| hamburger | | 369 |
| milk | | 95 |
| orange | | 65 |
| peanut butter sandwich | | 334 |
| pizza (1 slice) | | 378 |

12

Solve each problem.

Hank collects stamps. He buys a rare stamp for $71.93 and a package of stamps for $14.37. How much does Hank spend on stamps?

$$\begin{array}{r} \overset{1\ 1}{\$71.93} \\ +\ \$14.37 \\ \hline \$86.30 \end{array} \textbf{stamps}$$

**1.** At the toy store, Jill spends $95.38 for a doll. Carrie spends $42.69 less than Jill for a doll. How much does Carrie spend?

**2.** Hector buys a model car for $24.98. Then, he spends $18.39 on supplies to build the model car. How much does Hector spend altogether?

**3.** Mike collects baseball cards. He spends $58.27 on a rookie card. Then, he spends $74.93 on his favorite pitcher's card. How much does Mike spend on baseball cards in all?

**4.** Jack collects aluminum cans for recycling. He earns $23.79 in March and $39.08 in April. How much more money did Jack earn in April than in March?

Word Problems Grade 4—RBP0717

# Collecting Collectibles

Solve each problem.

1. John buys a painting for his collection. He spends $83.67. He gives the clerk $100.00. How much money does he get back?

2. Anne and Jim collect watches. Anne buys a watch for $58.48. Jim pays $39.37 more for his watch. How much does Jim pay?

3. Maria collects stickers. She spends $2.93 at the first store. She spends $12.43 at the second store. How much does Maria spend altogether?

4. Lori wants 2 packs of basketball cards and a new jersey. The card packs cost $3.53 each. The jersey costs $27.95. Lori has $35. Does she have enough?

**Did you know?**

If you had 10 billion $1 bills and spent one every second of every day, it would take 317 years for you to go broke.

14

Solve each problem.

Annie has $4.15 left in her purse. She spent $6.79 on party favors and $12.85 on decorations. How much did she have to start with?

```
  1 1 1
 $4.15
 $6.79
+ $12.85
 $23.79
```

**1.** Mia has $15.50 left in her pocket. She spent $2.75 on paper cups and $7.45 on punch. How much did she have to start with?

**2.** Chester had $58.25 in his wallet. He spent $6.78 on ice cream and $11.66 on a cake. His friend paid Chester $4.25 that he owed him. How much does Chester have in his wallet now?

**3.** Kim spends $4.83 on party favors. Then, she spends $11.77 on pizza and $27.98 for a present. If Kim started with $60.00, how much does she have now?

**4.** Spencer spends $6.77 for paper plates and $19.45 for ice cream. If he pays with a $50.00 bill, how much change will he get back?

© Rainbow Bridge Publishing

Word Problems Grade 4—RBP0717

# Party Plans

Solve each problem.

1. Suzie buys 349 cupcakes. She gives 102 to her neighbor. Then, she buys 283 more cupcakes. How many cupcakes does she have now?

2. Caroline spends $16.55 on soda and $22.49 on cake. Matt spends $42.85 on party favors and $17.45 on soda. How much more does Matt spend than Caroline?

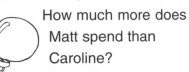

3. Lucy spends $14.12 on red balloons and $6.39 on blue balloons. Sean spends $7.43 on red balloons and $19.38 on yellow balloons. How much more does Sean spend than Lucy?

4. Eric spends $15.99 for pizza and $8.99 for soda. If he gives the cashier $30.00, how much change does he get back?

---

## Did you know?

Long ago, the measurement of a "foot" was based on the size of a human foot. A yard used to be the length from your nose to your fingertip. An acre was the amount of land an ox could plow in one day.

16

# People Populations

*Remember... When you round numbers, look at the number that follows the number you are rounding. For example, when rounding to the nearest ten, if the number you are rounding is followed by 5 or more, you round the number up. If the number you are rounding is followed by 4 or fewer, you round the number down.*

---

In Ashley's school there are 42 students who have computers.

42 rounded to the nearest 10 = **40**

---

Round each number to the nearest ten.

**1.** The chess club has 39 members.

**2.** In Jay's class, 24 students like to go bowling.

Round each number to the nearest thousand.

**3.** Newton County has a population of 4,700.

**4.** Randy's school has 2,230 people with blond hair.

Round each number to the nearest hundred.

**5.** At Hill Elementary, there are 369 students who have blue eyes.

**6.** The city of Daviston has 720 teachers.

**7.** In Marc's school, 412 students have pets.

---

**Did you know?**

According to the official census, the U.S. population in 2000 was 281,421,906. California is the state with the largest population.

Word Problems Grade 4—RBP0717

# Rock the Vote

Solve each problem.

Twenty-two people voted for fish as their favorite pet. Three times as many people voted for dogs. How many people voted altogether?

```
  22        66
x  3      + 22
  66        88  people
```

1. Marcus was elected president of the Wildlife Preservation Club. He got 7 times as many votes as his opponent. If his opponent got 65 votes, how many votes did Marcus get?

2. Sixty-four students voted for Murray. Two times as many students voted for Webster. How many students voted altogether?

3. The California candidate got 6 times as many votes as the Florida candidate. The Florida candidate got 85 votes. How many votes did the California candidate get?

4. Tiffany polled her class to see what their favorite kind of soda was. Eight times as many students voted for grape as orange soda. Forty-three students voted for orange soda. How many students voted altogether?

# Rock the Vote

Solve each problem.

1. Gina's class voted on their favorite type of vehicle. Trucks got 8 times as many votes as cars did. If cars got 35 votes, how many votes did trucks get?

2. Paige ran for class president. Five times as many students voted for Paige as for her opponent. Seventy-three students voted for her opponent. How many more students voted for Paige than for her opponent?

3. Grantsville's governor received 3 times as many votes as Maxfield's governor. Maxfield's governor received 790 votes. How many people voted altogether?

4. Six times as many people voted in the 2002 election as in the 1997 election. If 162 people voted in the 1997 election, how many people voted in both elections?

**Did you know?**

The shortest president of the United States was James Madison. He was 5 feet 4 inches tall. The tallest was Abraham Lincoln at 6 feet 4 inches.

Word Problems Grade 4—RBP0717

Solve each problem.

**1.** Otto's Car Lot sells 6 times as many cars as trucks. They sell 156 trucks. How many more cars than trucks do they sell?

**2.** Morgan spends 9 times more on tires than car polish. If he spends $4.88 on car polish, how much does he spend altogether?

**3.** On the car lot there are 8 times as many red cars as white cars. There are 347 white cars. How many cars are on the car lot altogether?

**4.** Denzel sees 5 times as many sport utility vehicles as sports cars. Denzel sees 253 sports cars. How many more sport utility vehicles than sports cars does Denzel see?

---

**Did you know?**

The oldest race for solar-powered cars is the World Solar Challenge held in Australia since 1987. The race is 1,800 miles long. In 2001, a Dutch team won with an average speed of 57 miles per hour.

# What's the Score?

Solve each problem.

1. The Panthers scored 7 times as many points as the Bears. If the Bears scored 89 points, how many more points did the Panthers score than the Bears?

2. The Tigers scored 4 times as many goals in June as in July. The Tigers scored 56 goals in July. How many goals did the Tigers score in both June and July?

3. Mark scored 8 times as many points as Tyler. Tyler scored 349 points. How many more points did Mark score than Tyler?

4. Peter spent 3 times as much on season tickets as Jan did. If Jan spent $73.43, how much more did Peter spend?

**Did you know?**

In 1922, the Chicago Cubs beat the Philadelphia Phillies 26 to 23. That's 49 total runs, the most ever scored in a major league baseball game.

21

# Two Scoops, Please

Use the circle graph to answer the questions.

Lisa's class members voted on their favorite flavors of ice cream. Use the circle graph to answer the questions.

30% chocolate

42% vanilla

10% rocky road

18% strawberry

1. Which flavor of ice cream received the highest number of votes?

2. What percentage of students voted for strawberry ice cream as their favorite flavor?

3. Which flavor of ice cream did 10 percent of the students vote for as their favorite?

4. What was the total percentage of students that liked either chocolate or strawberry best?

# Two Scoops, Please

Use the line graph to answer the questions.

**1.** How many gallons of ice cream were sold in January?

**2 gallons**

### Ice Cream Sales

(Bar graph — Gallons Sold vs. Jan., Feb., Mar., Apr., May, June)

| Month | Gallons Sold |
|-------|--------------|
| Jan. | 2 |
| Feb. | 6 |
| Mar. | 4 |
| Apr. | 3 |
| May | 9 |
| June | 7 |

**1.** Which month had the highest sales?

**2.** In which month were 4 gallons sold?

**3.** Which month had the lowest sales?

**4.** What was the total number of gallons of ice cream sold in February and March?

Word Problems Grade 4—RBP0717

# Adopt-a-Pet

Answer each question using the graph.

What is being compared on this graph?

**gerbils and guinea pigs sold**

**Pets Sold**

**KEY** = gerbils = guinea pigs

|  | Monday | Tuesday | Wednesday |
|---|---|---|---|
| 24 | | | |
| 20 | | | gerbils |
| 16 | gerbils | | gerbils |
| 12 | gerbils | gerbils | gerbils, guinea pigs |
| 8 | gerbils, guinea pigs | gerbils | gerbils, guinea pigs |
| 4 | gerbils, guinea pigs | gerbils, guinea pigs | gerbils, guinea pigs |

1. How many gerbils did the pet store sell on Tuesday?

2. On which day of the week were the most gerbils sold?

3. What was the total number of gerbils and guinea pigs sold on Wednesday?

4. On which day of the week did the pet store sell 8 guinea pigs?

# Adopt-a-Pet

Answer each question using the graph.

What is being compared on this graph?

**dogs and cats adopted**

**Pets Adopted**

**KEY** = dogs  = cats

| | April | May | June |
|---|---|---|---|
| 12 | | | |
| 10 | | | |
| 8 | | | cats |
| 6 | dogs | dogs | cats |
| 4 | dogs cats | dogs | dogs cats |
| 2 | dogs cats | dogs cats | dogs cats |
| | April | May | June |

1. How many cats were adopted in April?

2. How many dogs were adopted in June?

3. In which month were the most cats adopted?

4. How many more dogs than cats were adopted in May?

Word Problems Grade 4—RBP0717

Solve each problem.

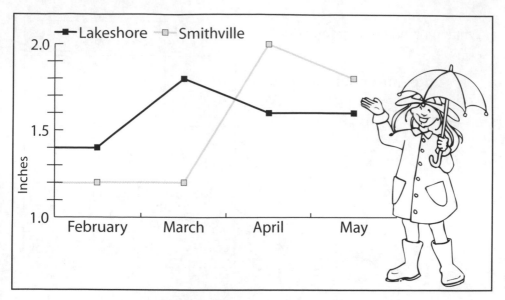

**1.** What was Lakeshore's average amount of rainfall?

**2.** In April and May, how many more inches of rain did Smithville get than Lakeshore?

**3.** What was Smithville's average amount of rainfall?

**4.** How many more inches of rain did Lakeshore get than Smithville altogether?

# Sports-R-Us

Solve each problem.

The Sports-R-Us store sells 2 types of tennis rackets. They have 58 of each type of tennis racket. How many tennis rackets does the store have altogether?

<sub>1</sub>
**58**
**x 2**
**116 tennis rackets**

---

**1.** Jack saw 4 times as many footballs as soccer balls in the store. Jack saw 34 soccer balls. How many footballs did Jack see?

**2.** In the winter season, the Sports-R-Us store sells 5 times as many snowboards as it sells during the summer season. The store sells 32 snowboards in the summer season. How many snowboards does the store sell in the winter season?

**3.** For each display, Tiffany put out 13 dumbbells. If there were 8 different displays, how many dumbbells did Tiffany put out?

**4.** Steven is checking his inventory. In the spring, he has 3 times as many pairs of skates as in the winter. If Steven has 56 pairs of skates in the winter, how many pairs of skates does he have in the spring?

27

# Magazine Mania

Solve each problem.

Casey sells 1,439 magazines every month.
How many magazines does
Casey sell in 9 months?

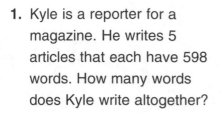

3 3 8
**1,439**
**x   9**
**12,951   magazines**

1. Kyle is a reporter for a magazine. He writes 5 articles that each have 598 words. How many words does Kyle write altogether?

2. Webster is a photographer for a magazine. The magazine uses 2 of his pictures on each page. If there are 139 pages in the magazine, how many pictures will Webster need to give them?

3. The Magazine Shop sold 8 times as many magazines as Montgomery's Bookstore. If Montgomery's Bookstore sold 2,587 magazines, how many magazines did the Magazine Shop sell?

4. Monica stocks shelves in the magazine store and puts 7 magazines in each box. Monica has 342 full boxes. How many magazines does Monica have?

# And the Winner Is...

Solve each problem.

| The California candidate got 34 times as many votes as the Florida candidate. The Florida candidate got 85 votes. How many votes did the California candidate get? | $\begin{array}{r} {}^{1}{}_{2}\phantom{0} \\ 85 \\ \times\ 34 \\ \hline 340 \\ \underline{255\phantom{0}} \\ 2{,}890 \text{ votes} \end{array}$ |
|---|---|

1. Twenty-seven students voted for Arthur. Thirty-one times as many students voted for Webster. How many students voted for Webster?

If I am elected president, I promise to outlaw peas!

2. Amy polled her class to see what the class's favorite kind of pizza was. Thirteen times as many students voted for pepperoni pizza as cheese pizza. Sixteen students voted for cheese pizza. How many students voted for pepperoni pizza?

3. Chad was elected treasurer of the Wildlife Preservation Club. He got 56 times as many votes as his opponent. If his opponent got 368 votes, how many votes did Chad get?

4. Brooke's fourth-grade class voted on their favorite book. *Harriet, the Spy* got 28 times as many votes as *The Boxcar Children*. If *The Boxcar Children* got 42 votes, how many votes did *Harriet, the Spy* get?

Word Problems Grade 4—RBP0717

# All Broken Up

Solve each problem.

Sara has 13 necklaces. Each necklace has 24 beads. She breaks 1 necklace and loses 14 beads. How many beads does Sara have left?

$$\begin{array}{r} \overset{1}{13} \\ \times\, 24 \\ \hline 52 \\ +\, 260 \\ \hline 312 \end{array}$$

$$\begin{array}{r} \overset{2\,1\,0\,1}{3\,\cancel{1}\,2} \\ -\, 14 \\ \hline 298 \text{ beads} \end{array}$$

1. Ed has 34 boxes of crayons. Each box has 24 crayons. Ed breaks 11 crayons while working on his project. How many crayons does Ed have left?

2. Mark has 48 cartons of eggs. Each carton has 12 eggs. He breaks 13 eggs. How many eggs does he have left?

3. Terry washes 28 loads of dishes. She washes 53 dishes in each load. She drops 16 dishes. How many dishes are left?

4. Elise is bottling root beer. She puts 83 bottles in each crate. She has 85 crates. She gives her friend 5 crates. How many bottles of root beer does Elise have left?

30

Solve each problem.

Alex buys 7 chocolate chip cookies for $1.24 each. How much does Alex spend on cookies?

```
  1 2
$1.24
x   7
$8.68
```

1. Jennifer works in a bakery. She earns $5.85 per hour. If Jennifer works 8 hours per day, how much does she earn in one day?

2. Louis buys 9 cakes for $16.48 each. How much money does Louis spend?

3. Shelly spends 6 times as much on pies for her party as Tom does. Tom spends $24.83. How much does Shelly spend on pies?

4. Madison, Gary, and Annie each buy one dozen doughnuts. One dozen doughnuts costs $7.59. How much do they spend on doughnuts altogether?

31

Solve each problem.

1. The bakery earns 7 times as much money selling bagels as it does selling cookies. If the bakery earns $58.39 selling cookies, how much money does the bakery earn selling bagels?

2. Roberto buys 4 boxes of éclairs for his party. Each box of éclairs costs $13.77. How much money does Roberto spend on éclairs?

3. Charlotte spends 7 times more money on peanut butter cookies than John. John spends $23.98 on peanut butter cookies. How much does Charlotte spend?

4. Lori earns $12 a week. She wants to buy 3 basketballs that cost $27.32 each. How much will the basketballs cost altogether? How many weeks will she need to work to buy them?

---

**Did you know?**

During the Civil War, the Bureau of Engraving and Printing printed paper money in denominations of 3 cents, 5 cents, 10 cents, 25 cents, and 50 cents. Paper money was printed when people hoarded coins, creating a drastic coin shortage.

# Bargain Buyers

Solve each problem using the information in the table.

| ITEM: | PRICE: |
|---|---|
| cereal | $3.75 |
| bananas | $.79 a pound |
| $\frac{1}{2}$ gallon of milk | $1.29 |
| 1 gallon of milk | $2.59 |
| soup | $2.55 |
| bread | $1.59 |
| peanut butter | $3.39 |

1. Kristy buys 2 boxes of cereal and 1 gallon of milk. She pays with a $20.00 bill. How much change should she get back?

2. Paul has $50.00 in his wallet. He buys 6 pounds of bananas, 2 loaves of bread, and 3 jars of peanut butter. How much does he have left?

3. Alan buys 3 gallons of milk and 7 boxes of cereal. Kesha buys 5 cans of soup and 2 loaves of bread. How much more does Alan spend than Kesha?

4. Allison buys 5 cans of soup and a jar of peanut butter. How much does she spend altogether?

33

Use the price list to solve each problem.

| ITEM | COST: |
|---|---|
| Adult admission | $6.75 |
| Child admission | $4.25 |
| Popcorn | $5.35 |
| Soda | $1.29 |
| Licorice | $2.49 |
| Lemon sours | $1.49 |
| Gumdrops | $2.39 |

1. Tia buys 3 adult admission tickets. Then, she buys a soda. How much does Tia spend altogether?

2. Marissa has $30.00 in her pocket. If she buys 3 children's tickets and 1 adult ticket, how much does she have left?

3. Kyle buys 4 boxes of licorice and a child's ticket. How much does he spend altogether?

4. Kara buys 7 packages of gumdrops. She hands the clerk $20.00. How much change does she get back?

Use the price list on page 34 to solve each problem.

1. Emmett buys 2 sodas, 1 popcorn, and 2 adult tickets. He pays with $25.00. How much change does he get back?

2. Alexis buys 3 sodas and 2 children's tickets. Megan buys 4 children's tickets and a package of licorice. How much more does Megan spend than Alexis?

3. Tanner buys 4 boxes of lemon sours and a soda. How much does he spend?

4. Nick buys 4 sodas and a child's ticket. How much does he spend in all?

**Did you know?**

*Reader's Digest* was the top-selling magazine in the U.S. in the year 2000. The magazine's circulation was 12,566,047. The second most popular magazine was *TV Guide*.

© Rainbow Bridge Publishing
Word Problems Grade 4—RBP0717

Solve each problem.

*Remember... The perimeter is the distance around a figure. To find the perimeter of a figure, add up the lengths of each side of the figure.*

| | |
|---|---|
| Jeremy is building a dog pen. Two of the sides are 17 feet long, and the other two sides are 21 feet long. How much fencing will Jeremy need? | $\begin{array}{r} {\scriptstyle 1} \\ 17 \\ 21 \\ 17 \\ + \ 21 \\ \hline 76 \end{array}$ **feet of fencing** |

1. Heather is putting tile around the edge of her swimming pool. Her swimming pool measures 20 feet by 16 feet. How many feet of tile will Heather have to put down?

2. Beth needs enough ribbon to go around the perimeter of her blanket. If the blanket measures 45 inches by 60 inches, how many inches of ribbon will Beth need to buy?

3. Kim is fencing an area in her yard. If two of the edges are 45 feet, and the other two edges are 57 feet, how many feet of fencing will Kim need?

4. Max is making a frame for a picture he painted. The picture is 36 inches by 18 inches. How many inches will his finished frame be?

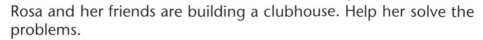
Rosa and her friends are building a clubhouse. Help her solve the problems.

*Remember... To find the area of a rectangular figure, multiply the length by the width.*

Rosa and Mike need to figure the area of the floor so they know how many boards to buy. If the floor is 8 feet by 12 feet, what is the area of the floor?

$$\begin{array}{r} 1\phantom{2} \\ 12 \\ \times\ 8 \\ \hline 96 \end{array}$$ **square feet**

1. Amy measures the area for the window. The window measures 16 inches wide and 21 inches tall. What is the area of the window?

2. Dylan wants to paint the back door to the clubhouse. The door is 56 inches tall and 32 inches wide. What is the area of the door?

3. Mike and Haley are working on the roof. They need to figure out the area so they will know how many shingles to buy. The roof is 108 inches by 156 inches. What is the area of the clubhouse roof?

4. Ashley wants to carpet a space in the clubhouse that is 32 inches by 59 inches. What is the area of the space she wants to carpet?

37

Solve each problem.

**1.** Lizzy is making a garden in her yard. What is the perimeter of her garden if each edge measures 36 feet?

**2.** Nancy is sewing trim around a tablecloth. If the tablecloth is 108 inches long and 72 inches wide, how many inches of trim does Nancy need?

**3.** Rosa makes a flower garden outside the clubhouse. The garden is 23 meters wide and 37 meters long. What is the area of Rosa's garden?

**4.** Dylan plants grass in a space behind the clubhouse that is 14 feet wide and 54 feet long. What is the area that Dylan plants?

---

**Did you know?**

U.S. currency is 2.61 inches wide by 6.14 inches long and 0.0043 inches thick. If the bills printed each year were laid end to end, they would stretch around the earth's equator about 24 times. Larger-sized notes in circulation before 1929 were 3.125 inches by 7.4218 inches.

Solve each problem.

*Remember... The perimeter is the distance around a figure. To find the perimeter of a figure, add up the lengths of each side of the figure.*

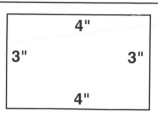

4"

3"                    3"

4"

**4" + 4" + 3" + 3" = 14 inches**

---

1. Jon and Kyle are putting tile around their bathtubs. Jon's area measures 78 inches by 62 inches. Kyle's area measures 69 inches by 53 inches. Who will need more tile, Jon or Kyle? How many more inches of tile will he need?

2. Melanie is buying trim to go around her rug. If two of the edges are 15 inches and the other two edges are 37 inches, how many inches of trim will she need? If trim costs 25¢ per inch, how much will she spend?

3. Lizzy is planting grass in her yard. She plants two places. The first measures 12 feet by 14 feet. The second measures 34 feet by 28 feet. What is the perimeter of the areas combined?

4. Ben is fencing a dog pen. Two of the sides are 55 feet, and the other two sides are 68 feet. How much fencing will Blake need? If fencing costs 6 cents per foot, how much will Ben spend?

Solve each problem.

*Remember... To find the area of a rectangular figure, multiply the length by the width.*

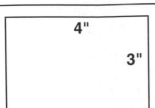

4"

3"

**4" x 3" = 12 square inches**

**1.** Rosa is planting wildflower seed. One bag of seed covers 6 square feet. If Rosa plants an area that is 36 feet by 14 feet, how many bags of seed will she need to buy?

**2.** Heather plants 134 flowers. Dylan plants 7 times as many flowers as Heather. How many more flowers did Dylan plant than Heather?

**3.** Steve plants 8 times as many marigolds as petunias. If Steve plants 65 petunias, how many flowers does Steve plant in all?

**4.** Haley sells 98 flats of pansies. If Haley sells 9 times as many geraniums as pansies, how many flowers does she sell altogether?

# Field Trip Fun

Solve each problem.

The fourth grade is going on a field trip to the zoo. There are 108 students and 3 buses. How many students are on each bus?

**108 ÷ 3 = 36 students**

1. The class visits the reptile house at the zoo. There are 245 reptiles. Each cage holds 5 reptiles. How many cages are there?

2. Robin's class takes a field trip to the museum. Robin sees 116 exhibits total. Each room has 4 exhibits in it. How many rooms does Robin go through?

3. Adrian's class is going to the theater. Half of the group goes into theater A. The other half of the group goes into theater B. If there are 114 students, how many students are in each theater?

4. Dan's class visits the natural history museum. The class sees 222 relics. If there are 6 relics in each room, how many rooms does the museum have?

Word Problems Grade 4—RBP0717

# Perfect Packaging

Solve each problem.

Kay has 300 eggs in cartons. There are 12 eggs in each carton. How many cartons will Kay have if she gives 7 cartons to her neighbor?

$$300 \div 12 = 25$$

$$\begin{array}{r} 25 \\ -\ 7 \\ \hline 18 \end{array} \textbf{ cartons}$$

1. Henry has 342 marbles. If there are 9 marbles in each bag, how many bags does Henry have? How many bags will he have if he gives 15 bags to his brother?

2. Grace orders 5 boxes of toothbrushes. If she has 135 toothbrushes altogether, how many are in each box? How many toothbrushes will she have left if she gives 2 boxes to her dentist?

3. Mario orders 595 candy bars. He has 7 boxes. How many candy bars are in each box? How many candy bars will he have left if he gives 3 boxes to his friend?

4. Peter has 135 books. If they are in 3 boxes, how many books are in each box? How many books will he have left if he donates 1 box of books to the library?

# Happy Campers

Solve each problem.

1. There are 544 marshmallows. Kelly drops 16. If there are 66 people to share the remaining marshmallows, how many will each camper get?

2. There are 61 campers. Nine go home early. If 13 people sleep in 1 tent, how many tents will the campers need?

3. The candy jar has 251 pieces of candy. Ryan adds 31 pieces of candy to it. If the candy is divided equally between 47 campers, how many pieces will each camper get?

4. There are 204 campers. Sixteen more campers come at night. If there are 55 tents, how many campers are in each tent?

## Did you know?

How about some winter camping? The coldest temperatures in the United States were recorded in Alaska (–80°F), Montana (–70°F), and Utah (–69°F).

Word Problems Grade 4—RBP0717

Solve each problem.

---

The hotel has 243 rooms. If each floor has 27 rooms, how many floors are in the hotel?

$$243 \div 27 = 9 \text{ floors}$$

---

1. James and his friends are at the Rent-a-Car lot. There are 392 cars. Each row has 56 cars. How many rows of cars are on the lot?

2. Kim flies to California. There are 144 passengers on her flight and 48 rows of seats. How many seats are in each row?

3. Lucy and her friends eat lunch at an Italian restaurant. The restaurant can seat 190 people. If there are 38 tables, how many people does each table seat?

4. Abby and her friends are visiting an amusement park. Their favorite ride, the Tidal Wave, holds 74 people. If 2 people fit in a car, how many cars are there on the ride?

Solve each problem.

1. Heather's class goes to a farm. At the farm, the class goes for a wagon ride. There are 105 students. If the wagon holds 7 students, how many trips will the wagon need to make so everyone gets a ride?

2. At the history museum, Danny's class breaks up into groups of 8 to look at the exhibits. If there are 168 students, how many groups are there?

3. Penny wants some marigold plants. She spends $18.41 on 7 potted marigolds. How much does each potted marigold cost?

4. Eric needs a big bag of dirt. He finds a 5-pound bag of dirt on sale for $7.80. What is the cost per pound for the bag of dirt?

I'm growing a row of numbers.

**Did you know?**

*Star Wars: Episode I—The Phantom Menace* earned 431 million dollars in ticket sales. *Toy Story 2* earned 245.9 million dollars, and *The Lion King* earned 312.9 million dollars in ticket sales.

Solve each problem.

---

Pam's favorite flowers are daisies. Pam spends $7.88 on 4 bunches of daisies. How much does each bunch cost?

**$7.88 ÷ 4 = $1.97**

---

1. Todd buys 7 long-stem roses. Todd spends $6.51 on the roses. How much does each rose cost?

2. Jada wants some purple flowers. She buys a 6 pack of petunias for $4.32. How much does each petunia plant cost?

3. The plant nursery has a sale on geraniums. Lance buys a case with 9 geraniums for $12.51. How much does each geranium cost?

4. Marie buys an 8-pound bag of plant fertilizer for $19.92. What is the cost per pound for the plant fertilizer?

Rainbow Bridge Publishing

Word Problems Grade 4—RBP0717

# Filling Flowerpots

Solve each problem.

1. Penny spends $13.65 on 7 potted marigolds. Judy buys 8 marigolds. How much does Judy spend?

2. Todd buys 8 long-stem roses. Todd spends $10.00 on the roses. He sells 2 of the roses for the same price he paid. How much does he earn?

3. Max buys 9 pounds of dirt for $22.95 to fill his flowerpots. Spencer buys 4 pounds. How much does Spencer spend on dirt?

4. Pam spends $9.00 on 4 bunches of daisies. Pam goes back to the store and buys 2 more bunches. How much does she pay?

**Did you know?**

There are about 250,000 species of flowering plants on Earth. More than half of the world's plant and animal species are found in tropical rain forests.

# Sea Explorers

Solve each problem.

Amy saw 6 times as many tropical fish as sea turtles. If she saw 17 sea turtles, how many sea turtles and tropical fish did she see total?

17
x 6
102 **tropical fish**
+ 17
119 **sea turtles and tropical fish**

**1.** Rex has 10 white seashells, 23 pink seashells, and 21 brown seashells. If he divides his seashells equally between 3 friends, how many seashells will each friend get?

**2.** Divers saw 88 tropical fish on Tuesday, 96 fish on Wednesday, and 32 fish on Thursday. What was the average number of fish the divers saw during the 3 days?

**3.** Max saw 4 times as many sand dollars as starfish. If he saw 51 starfish, how many sand dollars and starfish did Max see altogether?

**4.** A blue whale traveled 495 feet the first time it was sighted. The second time it was sighted, the blue whale had traveled 6 times as far as the first time. How far did the blue whale travel altogether?

48

Solve each problem.

**1.** A dolphin swam 587 yard on Monday. It swam 154 yards on Tuesday and 284 yards on Wednesday. What was the average number of yards it swam for the 3 days?

**2.** Sam has 26 yellow fish, 19 blue fish, and 43 orange fish. He has 8 fish tanks. If he divides the fish equally between each tank, how many fish are in each tank?

**3.** Alexis collected 518 seashells. Mia collected 5 times as many seashells as Alexis. How many seashells did Alexis and Mia collect altogether?

**4.** Lizzie saw 9 times as many starfish as sea urchins. If she saw 48 sea urchins, how many starfish and sea urchins did she see altogether?

**Did you know?**

The world's biggest ship is the *Jahre Viking*. It is a 1,502 foot long supertanker that can hold 4.2 million barrels of oil (1,502 feet is longer than the Empire State Building is tall!).

Word Problems Grade 4—RBP0717

# Lemonade Stand

Solve each problem.

Jessica uses 16 ounces of sugar in her lemonade recipe. If she makes 9 batches, how much sugar does she need?

$$\begin{array}{r} 5 \\ 16 \\ \times\ 9 \\ \hline 144 \end{array}$$ **ounces**

1. Mario sells 324 glasses of lemonade for 3¢ each. How much money does he earn?

2. Jamie sells 21 glasses of lemonade every day. If she sells lemonade for a week, how many glasses will she sell?

3. Tracy has 245 gallons of lemonade. She divides the lemonade into 5-gallon pitchers. How many pitchers can she fill?

4. Samantha buys 27 lemons for 9¢ each. How much money does Samantha spend?

Solve each problem.

1. Norman has 35 ounces of lemonade. He pours it into 5-ounce cups. How many cups of lemonade does he have?

2. Tyler spends 7¢ each for paper cups. If he buys 1,394 cups, how much money does he spend?

3. Kim sells lemonade for a week. Each day she earns $23.49. How much does she earn for the entire week?

4. Jasmine has 128 ounces of lemonade. She divides it equally into 8-ounce glasses. How many glasses of lemonade does Jasmine have?

**Did you know?**

The United States had half-cent, two-cent, and three-cent coins until the 1860s.

Word Problems Grade 4—RBP

# For Rent

Solve each problem.

There are 4 times as many apartments with carpet as apartments without carpet. If there are 259 apartments without carpet, how many apartments are there total?

$$
\begin{array}{r}
259 \\
\times\ \ 4 \\
\hline
1{,}036 \text{ apartments with carpet} \\
+\ 259 \\
\hline
1{,}295 \text{ apartments total}
\end{array}
$$

1. Jean pays 4 times as much rent as Peter. If Peter pays $853.00, how many more dollars does Jean pay than Peter?

2. There are 2,143 people in the Sandstone Apartments that own pets. There are 5 times as many people that don't own pets. How many people are in the Sandstone Apartments altogether?

3. Jasper's grandma gave him $345.00 for his birthday. He pays $32.50 for his bills each month. If he pays his bills for 9 months, how much money will he have left?

4. There are 4,297 renters in the Peachtree apartment building. There are 7 times as many renters in the Applewood apartment building. How many more renters are in the Applewood apartment building than the Peachtree apartment building?

# School Supplies

Solve each problem.

> Marcy buys rulers for her class. Each box has 8 rulers. How many boxes does Marcy need if there are 85 students in her class?
>
> ### $85 \div 8 = 10 +$ remainder of 5
> ### 11 boxes

1. Craig has $37. He buys bottles of glue for $2 each. How many bottles of glue can Craig buy?

2. Justin buys notebooks for all 159 students in his class. If each carton contains 7 notebooks, how many cartons does Justin need to buy to give one notebook to each student?

3. Penny brings candy for the class. Each package of candy has 9 pieces. There are 67 students in her class. How many packages of candy does Penny need to bring?

4. Sam shares stickers with his class. Each sticker sheet has 5 stickers. If Sam's class has 32 people, how many sheets of stickers does Sam need?

Word Problems Grade 4—RB

Solve each problem.

1. Chloe has $15 to spend on pencils. Each box of pencils costs $2. How many boxes of pencils can Chloe buy? How much money does Chloe have left after she buys the pencils?

2. There are 149 people in Ross's class. Ross buys erasers for each of the students. Erasers are sold 4 to a package. How many packages of erasers does Ross need to buy?

3. Janice has $269 to spend on books. Each book costs $8. How many books can Janice buy?

4. Lori needs athletic socks. They come in packs of 3 for $7. Lori has $25. How many packs of socks can she buy? How much money will she have left?

## Did you know?

The Bureau of Engraving and Printing produces 37 million bills per day with a face value of approximately $696 million. Forty-five percent of the notes printed are $1 bills.

Solve each problem.

*Remember...*
* *If you change a larger unit to a smaller unit (yards to feet), you multiply.*
* *If you change a smaller unit to a larger unit (inches to feet), you divide.*

     *12 inches = 1 foot*     *3 feet = 1 yard*     *36 inches = 1 yard*

---

Pam needs 36 inches of rope. How many yards does she need to buy?

**36 ÷ 12 = 3 feet = 1 yard**

---

1. Jason needs 180 inches of string for his project. How many yards should he buy?

2. Maggie is carpeting her hall. The length of the hall is 14 feet. Carpet is sold by the yard. How many yards does Maggie need to buy so she will have enough?

3. Kristen is going to put together a puzzle that is 72 inches wide. Her table is 5 feet wide. How many inches wide is Kristen's table? Will her puzzle fit on the table?

4. The toy racetrack is 60 inches long. How many feet is the toy racetrack?

Word Problems Grade 4—RBP0

# Kitchen Conversions

Solve each problem.

*Remember...*
- *If you change a larger unit to a smaller unit (tablespoon to teaspoon), you multiply.*
- *If you change a smaller unit to a larger unit (quart to gallon), you divide.*

*1 tablespoon = 3 teaspoons   1 pint = 2 cups*
*1 quart = 2 pints     1 gallon = 4 quarts    1 pound = 16 ounces*

Maria's jam recipe calls for 8 pints of chopped fruit. How many quarts of chopped fruit does she need?

**8 ÷ 2 = 4 quarts**

1. Ben needs 16 quarts of punch for the party. How many gallons of punch does Ben need to buy?

2. James is making cookies for a bake sale at his school. He uses 64 ounces of chocolate chips in his recipe. How many pounds of chocolate chips does he use?

3. Mario needs 3 gallons of soup for his party. The restaurant packages the soup in quart bottles. How many bottles does he have to pick up?

4. Angela is making a triple-layer chocolate cake, and her recipe calls for 2 tablespoons of vanilla. Angela only has a teaspoon to measure with. How many teaspoons should she use?

# Racetrack Racers

Solve each problem.

*Remember... When the denominators are the same, subtract the numerators and then the whole numbers.*

Duane watches a car race. The red race car drives $7\frac{1}{10}$ miles. The silver race car drives $9\frac{6}{10}$ miles. How many more miles does the silver race car drive than the red race car?

$$9\frac{6}{10}$$
$$-\ 7\frac{1}{10}$$
$$\mathbf{2\frac{5}{10}\ miles}$$

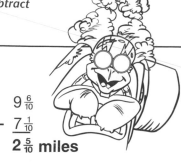

1. The brown horse runs $\frac{3}{12}$ of a mile farther than the black horse. The black horse runs $15\frac{4}{12}$ of a mile. How far does the brown horse run?

2. Karla runs $6\frac{5}{16}$ miles, and Jason runs $11\frac{4}{16}$ miles. How many miles do Karla and Jason run altogether?

3. Toby competes in a bicycle race. On the first day of the race, he rides $17\frac{4}{23}$ miles. On the second day of the race, he rides $22\frac{12}{23}$ miles. How far does Toby ride altogether?

4. John runs $10\frac{3}{6}$ meters. Erica runs $11\frac{5}{6}$ meters. How much farther does Erica run?

Word Problems Grade 4—RBP0

# Birthday Blast

Ryan is making a birthday cake for his friend's birthday. Help him solve each problem.

*Remember... When adding or subtracting fractions with different denominators, first find the lowest common denominator for the fractions. Convert the fractions, and then add or subtract the numerators.*

Ryan needs $6\frac{3}{4}$ cups of flour for his recipe. When he measures the flour in his bag, he only has $3\frac{2}{3}$ cups of flour. How much more flour does Ryan need for his recipe?

$$6\frac{3}{4} = 6\frac{9}{12}$$
$$-3\frac{2}{3} = -3\frac{8}{12}$$
$$\overline{\quad\quad\quad 3\frac{1}{12} \text{ cups of flour}}$$

1. Next, the recipe says to sift together $\frac{5}{8}$ teaspoon of baking powder with $\frac{1}{3}$ teaspoon of salt. How many teaspoons does Ryan sift altogether?

2. Ryan adds $1\frac{2}{3}$ cups of sugar and realizes he put in too much sugar. He takes out $\frac{1}{4}$ cup of sugar from the mixing bowl. How much sugar does Ryan use in the recipe?

3. Applesauce is the next ingredient Ryan needs to add. He measures $\frac{5}{8}$ cup and then adds $\frac{1}{9}$ cup. How much applesauce does Ryan add altogether?

4. Ryan has a full carton of 12 eggs. He uses $\frac{1}{3}$ of the carton. How many eggs does Ryan have left?

Solve each problem.

1. Mindy drives her car $35\frac{6}{12}$ times around the racetrack. Shannon drives her car $21\frac{4}{12}$ times around the racetrack. How many more times does Mindy drive her car around the racetrack than Shannon?

2. Jay swims $\frac{3}{10}$ of a mile farther than Randy. If Randy swims $2\frac{4}{10}$ miles, how far does Jay swim?

3. Ryan bakes the cake for $25\frac{5}{12}$ minutes. He decides it needs to bake longer. He bakes it for another $2\frac{3}{6}$ minutes. How long does the cake bake altogether?

4. Next, Ryan frosts the birthday cake. He uses $1\frac{5}{6}$ cups of frosting and then adds another $\frac{3}{8}$ cup of frosting. How much frosting does Ryan use altogether?

---

**Did you know?**

The average speed of a car driving in the Indianapolis 500 race in 2001 was 131.294 miles per hour.

Word Problems Grade 4—RBP071

# Going the Distance

Solve each problem.

Henry runs three and six-tenths miles. Write the decimal number that shows how many miles Henry runs.

**3.6**

1. Dotty scores twenty-three and two-tenths points. Write the decimal number that shows how many points Dotty scores.

2. Jacob's kite flies sixty-nine and five-hundredths yards. Write the decimal number that shows how many yards Jacob's kite flies.

3. Becky swims two and thirty-five-hundredths miles. Write the decimal number that shows how many miles Becky swims.

4. Max scored twenty-eight and two-tenths points. Write the decimal number that shows how many points Max scored.

www.summerbridgeactivities.com

Solve each problem.

**1.** Jackson drives fifty-eight and forty-five hundredths miles. Write the decimal number that shows how many miles Jackson drives.

**2.** Brad throws the ball twenty-one and three-tenths feet. Write the decimal number that shows how many feet Brad throws the ball.

**3.** Claire jogs six and nine-tenths miles. Write the decimal number that shows how many miles Claire jogs.

**4.** Mitch earns ten and forty-five-thousandths points. Write the decimal number that shows how many points Mitch earns.

## Did you know?

The symbol for the Olympic Games is five rings. Each ring symbolizes a continent: Europe, Asia, Africa, Australia, and America. The blue, yellow, black, green, and red rings are linked together to represent the friendship of all people.

Word Problems Grade 4—RBP0717

# Car Craze

Solve each problem.

*Remember... To add and subtract decimals, you must first line up the decimal points. Put in zeros for any missing numbers. Add or subtract. Remember to put the decimal point in the answer.*

Eve drives 67.4 miles farther than Tyler. If Tyler drives 45.39 miles, how many miles does Eve drive?

$$\begin{array}{r} {}^{1}67.40 \\ +\ 45.39 \\ \hline 112.79 \end{array}$$ **miles**

1. In 2000, 47.8 percent of the cars sold in the U.S. were midsize cars. The percentage of small cars sold was 28.1 percent. How many more midsize cars than small cars were sold?

2. Brett drives 95.3 miles on Friday and 76.9 miles on Saturday. How many miles does Brett drive altogether?

3. In 1999, 16.5 percent of people in the U.S. bought luxury cars. That same year, 52.7 percent of the people in the U.S. bought midsize cars. What was the total percentage of people that bought either luxury cars or midsize cars?

4. Dean's truck gets 15.3 miles per gallon of gas. Christy's car gets 25.2 miles per gallon of gas. How many more miles per gallon does Christy's car get?

Solve each problem.

In 1996, the best time for the 400-meter hurdles was 47.54 seconds. The best time in 1980 was 48.70 seconds. How much faster was the time in 1996 than the time in 1980?

$$\begin{array}{r} {}^{6\,1}\\ 48.\cancel{7}0\\ -\,47.54\\ \hline 1.16 \textbf{ seconds} \end{array}$$

**1.** In the long jump, Carl Lewis had a distance of 8.50 meters in 1996. In 1936, Jesse Owens had a distance of 8.06 meters. How much farther did Carl Lewis jump than Jesse Owens?

**2.** U.S. speed skater Bonnie Blair won the Olympic gold medal for women's 500-meter speed skating in 1992 and 1994. In 1992, her time was 40.33 seconds. In 1994, her time was 39.25 seconds. How much faster was Bonnie's time in 1994 than her time in 1992?

**3.** In 2000, the 100-meter freestyle was completed in 48.30 seconds. In 1972, the 100-meter freestyle was completed in 51.22 seconds. How many seconds more did it take to complete the 100-meter freestyle in 1972?

**4.** The U.S. won gold medals in the women's 100-meter run in both 1996 and 2000. The winning time in 1996 was 10.94 seconds. The winning time in 2000 was 10.75 seconds. How much faster was the winning time in 2000?

Word Problems Grade 4—RBP0717

Use the information in the table to work each problem.

| CITY | INCHES OF RAINFALL IN JUNE |
|------|---------------------------|
| Charleston | 6.4 |
| Chicago | 3.4 |
| Hartford | 3.8 |
| Little Rock | 7.8 |
| Miami | 10.3 |
| San Antonio | 4.2 |

*The digits are really coming down today!*

1. What was the average amount of rainfall for Miami, San Antonio, and Hartford?

2. The temperature in Bismarck was 21 degrees. In Houston, the temperature was 3 times higher than the temperature in Bismarck. How many degrees higher was the temperature in Houston than Bismarck?

3. Seattle had 3 times as much rainfall as Chicago. How many inches of rain did Seattle and Chicago have altogether?

4. On Monday, the temperature in Salt Lake City was 91 degrees. On Tuesday, the temperature was 84 degrees, and on Wednesday it was 83 degrees. What was the average temperature for the 3-day period?

Use the information in the table on page 64 to work each problem.

**1.** Dallas had 1.4 inches less rainfall than San Antonio. Austin had 2.3 more inches of rainfall than Dallas. How many inches of rainfall did Dallas, San Antonio, and Austin get altogether?

**2.** What was the average amount of rainfall for Hartford and Little Rock?

**3.** If Savannah had 2 times more rainfall than Hartford, how much rainfall did Savannah and Hartford have altogether?

**4.** Portland had 3 times as much rainfall as Chicago. How many more inches of rainfall did Portland get than Chicago?

**Did you know?**

A bolt of lighting can generate up to a billion volts of electricity and heat up the air around it to a toasty 50,000°F!

© Rainbow Bridge Publishing

Word Problems Grade 4—RBP0717

# Basketball Scores

**10**

Solve each problem.

*Remember...*
- *The <u>range</u> is the difference between the highest number and the lowest number in the data.*
- *To calculate the <u>mean</u> (or average), add the list of numbers and then divide by the number of items.*
- *The <u>median</u> is the middle number that appears in the data.*
- *The <u>mode</u> is the number that appears most often in the data.*

> The Panthers kept track of their scores from their last seven basketball games.
> <u>Here are their scores:</u>
> 93, 90, 85, 85, 81, 71, 69

**1.** What is the range of the basketball scores?

**2.** What is the mode of the basketball scores?

**3.** What is the median of the basketball scores?

**4.** What is the mean of the basketball scores?

## Did you know?

Michael Jordan was the NBA scoring leader for ten seasons. In 1987, Jordan earned an average of 37.1 points per game.

# Cookie Crumbs

Sara's class voted on their favorite kind of cookie. Use the information to figure out how many voted for each cookie.

Ten fewer students voted for snickerdoodles than peanut butter.

Nineteen students voted for oatmeal.

Six more students voted for pumpkin than raisin.

Seven times as many students voted for chocolate chip as oatmeal.

Four more students voted for peanut butter than chocolate chip.

Eight times as many students voted for raisin as snickerdoodles.

| Cookie: | Number of votes: |
|---|---|
| chocolate chip | |
| snickerdoodles | |
| oatmeal | |
| peanut butter | |
| raisin | |
| pumpkin | |

Word Problems Grade 4—RBP0717

# Balloon Bunches

Zoe has a bunch of balloons. Use the information below to figure out how many of each color balloon she has and organize the information in the table.

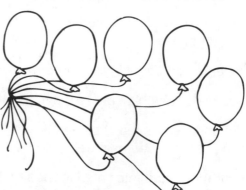

There are 15 green balloons.

There are 3 times as many yellow as green.

There are 22 more red than yellow.

There are 12 fewer blue than red.

There are 2 times as many orange as blue.

There are 3 more purple than green.

| Color: | Number of balloons: |
|---|---|
| orange | |
| yellow | |
| red | |
| purple | |
| blue | |
| green | |

# Balloon Bunches

Use the table on page 68 to solve each problem.

1. If there are 6 fewer black balloons than orange balloons, how many black and orange balloons are there altogether?

2. Megan has 34 red balloons, 48 green balloons, and 12 yellow balloons. If she divides her balloons equally between 5 friends, how many balloons will each friend get?

3. Andi buys 8 times as many red balloons as purple balloons. Then, she buys 2 times as many yellow balloons as red balloons. She buys 14 purple balloons. If she pays 6¢ for each balloon, how much does she spend altogether?

4. Stuart has 69 balloons. Thirteen of his balloons pop! Then 4 balloons float away. If he divides the remaining balloons equally between 4 friends, how many balloons will each friend get?

Word Problems Grade 4—RBP0717

## Critical Thinking Skills

## Team Spirit

Read each problem carefully and decide which information is needed to solve it. Then, work each problem.

Go Team!

1. Gary ran 14 yards Tuesday and 34 yards Wednesday. On Thursday, he ran 9 yards less than he ran on Wednesday. His brother ran 22 yards on Friday. How many yards did Gary run altogether?

2. The Bears scored 187 points during March. The Panthers scored 3 times as many points as the Bears. The Rams scored 115 points. How many points did the Bears and Panthers score altogether?

3. Emma ran 1.6 miles. Beth ran 2.5 miles. Greta ran 3 times as many miles as Beth. Lisa ran 4.3 miles. How many miles did Emma, Beth, and Greta run altogether?

4. Dennis kicked 6 times more footballs than soccer balls in the store. Dennis kicked 114 soccer balls. Tyler kicked 53 soccer balls. How many footballs and soccer balls did Dennis kick altogether?

www.summerbridgeactivities.com
© Rainbow Bridge Publishing

# Team Spirit

Read each problem carefully and decide which information is needed to solve it. Then, work each problem.

1. Lucy scored 5 times as many points as Ramona. Ramona scored 27 points. Erica scored 9 fewer points than Lucy. How many more points did Lucy score than Ramona?

2. Stephanie spent 14 times as much on her basketball tickets as she did on her hot dog at the game. A pretzel costs $2.65. If she spent $2.15 on her hot dog, how much did she spend altogether?

3. Karl scored 16 points. Rick scored 24 more points than Karl. Alexis scored 38 points. Kim scored 15 fewer points than Rick. How many points were scored altogether?

4. The Tigers hit 9 times as many home runs as the Wolves during the season. The Bulls hit 29 home runs. The Wolves hit 37 home runs. How many more home runs did the Tigers hit than the Wolves?

Word Problems Grade 4—RBP0717

# Camping Adventures

Tyler and his family are going camping. Use the map to solve each problem.

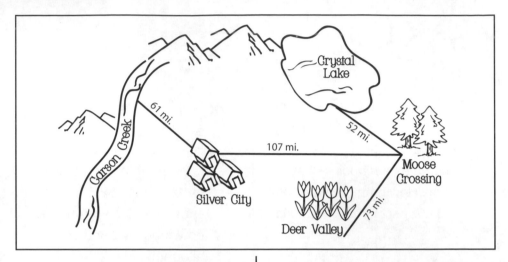

1. Tyler's family drove from Carson Creek to Crystal Lake. How many miles did they travel altogether?

2. If Tyler's family drove 55 miles per hour, how long did it take them to get to Crystal Lake?

3. If they get 22 miles per gallon of gas, how many gallons of gas did they use to get to Crystal Lake?

4. If gas costs $1.69 a gallon, how much did they spend on gas?

# Camping Adventures

Solve each problem. Use the map on page 72 if you need to.

1. Tyler and his sister see 3 times as many deer as moose. They see 13 moose. They also see 8 fewer bears than moose. How many animals did Tyler and his sister see altogether?

2. Haley's family drove from Deer Valley to Crystal Lake. Then they left Crystal Lake and drove to Silver City. How many miles did they travel altogether?

3. Haley hiked 4 times as many miles as her sister. Her sister hiked 14 miles. Haley's mom hiked 6 miles. How many miles did Haley's family hike altogether?

4. How many miles further is it from Carson Creek to Moose Crossing than from Deer Valley to Moose Crossing?

Word Problems Grade 4—RBP0717

# At the Amusement Park

Read each problem and decide if enough information is given to solve it. If there is enough information, solve the problem.

1. Justin buys 2 sodas for $1.85 and 6 tickets for $8.49. How much change does he get back?

2. Chloe buys 7 tickets for $0.79 each and a snow cone for $1.49. She gives the cashier $20.00. How much change does she get back?

3. Dana rides the carousel 9 times. One ride on the carousel takes 4 tickets. If one ticket costs 5¢, how much does Dana spend on carousel rides?

4. Miranda buys cotton candy and a hot dog. A slice of pizza costs $1.39. How much does Alex spend altogether?

# Answer Pages

**Page 3**
1. 53 black ants
2. 59 caterpillars
3. 61 spiders
4. 43 ladybugs

**Page 4**
1. 97 reptiles
3. 6,891 people
4. 111 pictures
5. 6,240 ounces of birdseed

**Page 5**
1. 37 bees
2. 150 cages
3. 40 butterflies
4. 419 feet

**Page 6**
1. 323 feet
2. 73 feet
3. 204 feet
4. 9,490 feet

**Page 7**
1. 7,628 feet
2. 5,425 seashells
3. 2,326 feet
4. 127 sea urchins

**Page 8**
1. 8,715 feet
2. 83 feet
3. 523 sea creatures
4. 1,984 fish

**Page 9**
1. 27 pictures of parks
2. 46 tourists
3. 239 postcards
4. 58 souvenirs

**Page 10**
1. 486 pieces
2. 157 visitors
3. 216 posters
4. 253 miles

**Page 11**
1. 368 pounds of soap
2. 150 brown socks
3. 30 loads
4. 26 socks

**Page 12**
1. 44 calories
2. 378 calories
3. 321 calories
4. 495 calories

**Page 13**
1. $52.69
2. $43.37
3. $133.20
4. $15.29

**Page 14**
1. $16.33
2. $97.85
3. $15.36
4. No (total cost is $35.01)

Word Problems Grade 4—RBP0717

# Answer Pages

**Page 15**
1. $25.70
2. $44.06
3. $15.42
4. $23.78

**Page 16**
1. 530 cupcakes
2. $21.26
3. $6.30
4. $5.02

**Page 17**
1. 40
2. 20
3. 5,000
4. 2,000
5. 400
6. 700
7. 400

**Page 18**
1. 455 votes
2. 192 students
3. 510 votes
4. 387 students

**Page 19**
1. 280 votes
2. 292 students
3. 3,160 people
4. 1,134 people

**Page 20**
1. 780 cars
2. $48.80
3. 3,123 cars
4. 1,012 sport utility vehicles

**Page 21**
1. 534 points
2. 280 goals
3. 2,443 points
4. $146.86

**Page 22**
1. vanilla
2. 18%
3. rocky road
4. 48%

**Page 23**
1. May
2. March
3. January
4. 10 gallons

**Page 24**
1. 4 gerbils
2. Wednesday
3. 32 gerbils and guinea pigs
4. Monday

**Page 25**
1. 4 cats
2. 4 dogs
3. June
4. 4 more dogs

**Page 26**
1. 1.6 inches
2. 0.6 inches
3. 1.55 inches
4. 0.2 inches

www.summerbridgeactivities.com

# Answer Pages

**Page 27**
1. 136 footballs
2. 160 snowboards
3. 104 dumbbells
4. 168 skates

**Page 28**
1. 2,990 words
2. 278 pictures
3. 20,696 magazines
4. 2,394 magazines

**Page 29**
1. 837 students
2. 208 students
3. 20,608 votes
4. 1,176 votes

**Page 30**
1. 805 crayons
2. 563 eggs
3. 1,468 dishes
4. 6,640 bottles

**Page 31**
1. $46.80
2. $148.32
3. $148.98
4. $22.77

**Page 32**
1. $408.73
2. $55.08
3. $167.86
4. $81.96; 7 weeks

**Page 33**
1. $9.91
2. $31.91
3. $18.09
4. $16.14

**Page 34**
1. $21.54
2. $10.50
3. $14.21
4. $3.27

**Page 35**
1. $3.57
2. $7.12
3. $7.25
4. $9.41

**Page 36**
1. 72 feet
2. 210 inches
3. 204 feet
4. 108 inches

**Page 37**
1. 336 square inches
2. 1,792 square inches
3. 16,848 square inches
4. 1,888 square inches

**Page 38**
1. 144 feet
2. 360 inches
3. 851 square meters
4. 756 square feet

# Answer Pages

**Page 39**
1. Jon, 36 inches
2. 104 inches, $26.00
3. 176 feet
4. 246 feet, $14.76

**Page 40**
1. 84 bags
2. 804 flowers
3. 585 flowers
4. 980 flats

**Page 41**
1. 49 cages
2. 29 rooms
3. 57 students
4. 37 rooms

**Page 42**
1. 38 bags, 23 bags
2. 27 toothbrushes, 81 toothbrushes
3. 85 candy bars, 340 candy bars
4. 45 books, 90 books

**Page 43**
1. 8 marshmallows
2. 4 tents
3. 6 pieces
4. 4 campers

**Page 44**
1. 7 rows
3. 3 seats
4. 5 people
5. 37 cars

**Page 45**
1. $0.93
2. $0.72
3. $1.39
4. $2.49

**Page 46**
1. 15 trips
2. 21 groups
3. $2.63
4. $1.56

**Page 47**
1. $15.60
2. $2.50
3. $10.20
4. $4.50

**Page 48**
1. 18 seashells
2. 72 fish
3. 255 starfish and sand dollars
4. 3,465 feet

**Page 49**
1. 341 yards
2. 11 fish
3. 3,108 seashells
4. 480 starfish and sea urchins

**Page 50**
1. 972¢ or $9.72
2. 147 glasses
3. 49 pitchers
4. 243¢ or $2.43

www.summerbridgeactivities.com

# Answer Pages

**Page 51**
1. 7 cups
2. 9,758¢ or $97.58
3. $164.43
4. 16 glasses

**Page 52**
1. $2,559
2. 12,858 people
3. $52.50
4. 25,782 renters

**Page 53**
1. 18 bottles, with $1 left over
2. 23 cartons
3. 8 packages
4. 7 sheets

**Page 54**
1. 7 boxes, with $1.00 left over
2. 38 packages
3. 33 books
4. 3 packs of socks, with $4 left over

**Page 55**
1. 5 yards
2. 5 yards
3. 60 inches, no
4. 5 feet

**Page 56**
1. 4 gallons
2. 4 pounds
3. 12 bottles
4. 6 teaspoons

**Page 57**
1. $15\frac{7}{12}$ miles
2. $17\frac{9}{16}$ miles
3. $39\frac{16}{23}$ miles
4. $1\frac{2}{6}$ meters

**Page 58**
1. $\frac{23}{24}$ teaspoon
2. $\frac{17}{12}$ or $1\frac{5}{12}$ cups
3. $\frac{53}{72}$ cup
4. $\frac{8}{12}$, 8 eggs, or $\frac{2}{3}$ of a carton

**Page 59**
1. $14\frac{2}{12}$ or $14\frac{1}{6}$ times
2. $2\frac{7}{10}$ miles
3. $27\frac{11}{12}$ minutes
4. $\frac{53}{24}$ or $2\frac{5}{24}$ cups

**Page 60**
1. 23.2
2. 69.05
3. 2.35
4. 28.2

**Page 61**
1. 58.45
2. 21.3
3. 6.9
4. 10.045

**Page 62**
1. 19.7 percent
2. 172.2 miles
3. 69.2 percent
4. 9.9 miles per gallon

**Page 63**
1. 0.44 meters
2. 1.08 seconds
3. 2.92 seconds
4. 0.19 seconds

**Page 64**
1. 6.1 inches
2. 42 degrees
3. 13.6 inches
4. 86 degrees

**Page 65**
1. 12.1 inches
2. 5.8 inches
3. 11.4 inches
4. 6.8 inches

**Page 66**
1. 24
2. 85
3. 85
4. 82

**Page 67**
1. chocolate chip—133 votes
2. snickerdoodles—127 votes
3. oatmeal—19 votes
4. peanut butter—137 votes
5. raisin—1,016 votes
6. pumpkin—1,022 votes

**Page 68**
1. 110 orange
2. 45 yellow
3. 67 red
4. 18 purple
5. 55 blue
6. 15 green

**Page 69**
1. 214 balloons
2. 18 balloons, with 4 left over
3. $21.00
4. 13 balloons

**Page 70**
1. 73 yards
2. 748 points
3. 11.6 miles
4. 798 balls

**Page 71**
1. 108 points
2. $32.25
3. 119 points
4. 296 home runs

**Page 72**
1. 220 miles
2. 4 hours
3. 10 gallons
4. $16.90

**Page 73**
1. 57 animals
2. 284 miles
3. 76 miles
4. 95 miles

**Page 74**
1. not enough information
2. $12.98
3. $1.80
4. not enough information